The Killing:
Meditations on the
Death of Christ

The Killing: Meditations on the Death of Christ

RICHARD HOLLOWAY

Foreword by the Archbishop of Canterbury

Darton, Longman & Todd
London

First published in 1984 by
Darton, Longman and Todd Ltd
89 Lillie Road, London SW6 1UD

Reprinted 1984 and 1985

British Library Cataloguing in Publication Data
Holloway, Richard
  The killing: meditations on the death of Christ.
  1. Jesus Christ—Crucifixion—Meditations
  I. Title
  232.9′63   BT450

ISBN 0 232 51593 X

Phototypeset by Input Typesetting Ltd, London SW19 8DR
Printed and bound in Great Britain by
Anchor Brendon Ltd, Tiptree, Essex

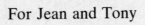

For Jean and Tony

The Killing

That was the day they killed the Son of God
On a squat hill-top by Jerusalem.
Zion was bare, her children from their maze
Sucked by the demon curiosity
Clean through the gates. The very halt and blind
Had somehow got themselves up to the hill.

After the ceremonial preparation,
The scourging, nailing, nailing against the wood,
Erection of the main-trees with their burden,
While from the hill rose an orchestral wailing,
They were there at last, high up in the soft spring day.
We watched the writhings, heard the moanings, saw
The three heads turning on their separate axles
Like broken wheels left spinning. Round his head
Was loosely bound a crown of plaited thorn
That hurt at random, stinging temple and brow
As the pain swung into its envious circle.
In front the wreath was gathered in a knot
That as he gazed looked like the last stump left
Of a death-wounded deer's great antlers. Some
Who came to stare grew silent as they looked,
Indignant or sorry. But the hardened old
And the hard-hearted young, although at odds
From the first morning, cursed him with one curse,

Having prayed for a Rabbi or an armed Messiah
And found the Son of God. What use to them
Was a God or a Son of God? Of what avail
For purposes such as theirs? Beside the cross-foot,
Alone, four women stood and did not move
All day. The sun revolved, the shadow wheeled,
The evening fell. His head lay on his breast,
But in his breast they watched his heart move on
By itself alone, accomplishing its journey,
Their taunts grew louder, sharpened by the knowledge
That he was walking in the part of death,
Far from their rage. Yet all grew stale at last,
Spite, curiosity, envy, hate itself,
They waited only for death and death was slow
And came so quietly they scarce could mark it.
They were angry then with death and death's deceit.

I was a stranger, could not read these people
Or this outlandish deity. Did a God
Indeed in dying cross my life that day
By chance, he on his road and I on mine?

Edwin Muir

Contents

Acknowledgements

As usual, I owe an enormous debt of gratitude to my wife, Jean, for her help in the production of this little book. She it was who transcribed the whole thing from tape recordings and then went on to correct the proofs of the final, edited version. For these and many other things I am deeply grateful to her. I am also very grateful to my secretary, Martha Mitchell, for typing the various drafts of the book. She, too, has my hearty thanks for her cheerful and uncomplaining labours. It is most kind of the Archbishop of Canterbury to take time out from all his other work to write a foreword for this book, and I am extremely grateful. Finally, I'd like to record my thanks to the editorial staff of Darton Longman and Todd for their unfailing helpfulness and courtesy.

Richard Holloway
The Church of the Advent
30 Brimmer Street
Boston, Massachusetts 02108

Thanks are due to the following for permission to reproduce extracts from copyright sources

Faber and Faber Ltd: *The Collected Poems of Edwin Muir*. Reprinted by permission.

Hodder and Stoughton Ltd: *The Unutterable Beauty* by G. A. Studdert Kennedy.

Oxford University Press: *The Poems of Gerald Manley Hopkins*, 4th edn., (1967) ed. W. H. Gardner and N. H. MacKenzie, published by Oxford University Press for the Society of Jesus.

S.P.C.K. *My God My Glory* by Eric Milner-White, 1967.

Foreword
by the Archbishop of Canterbury

I am an admirer of Richard Holloway's writing. He deals with the central themes of the Christian faith, as in this book about the Crucifixion, but he always writes with freshness and vigour and with a blessed freedom from stale ecclesiastical jargon.

The Killing is the work of a man who has not taken refuge in the niceties of textual scholarship. The tone is urgent and the question is not fudged – have we the grace and courage to be involved in the story of Christ, or are we mere onlookers and really disengaged?

The choice is presented with clarity, but in a way which is neither hectoring nor contemptuous. The author has too much human sympathy to ignore the allure and frequency of the temptation, even for believers, to idle in neutral in the face of the suffering Christ and his invitation that we should take up our own cross and follow Him.

If the Way of Christ has never frightened us, then it is possible that we have never understood the Scriptures. I hope that *The Killing* will help many to enter into the heart of the Mystery of the Cross, since this is the only preparation for seeing and receiving the depths of joy and hope that come with the Resurrection of Our Lord on Easter Day.

Lambeth Palace
4th October 1983

PART I

THE ACTORS

1

The Secret Admirer

When Jesus had spoken these words, he went forth with his disciples across the Kidron valley, where there was a garden, which he and his disciples entered. John 18:1

There is a popular Sunday newspaper in Britain which advertises itself with the slogan: 'All life is there.' I do not want to say anything about the quality of the newspaper, but I think it is a good slogan, and I would like to borrow it. What is more, I would like to use it as a motto for the New Testament: All life is *there*. The New Testament is about Jesus Christ and how people reacted to him, what they made of him, what they did to him. But Jesus Christ is not just a character from history, someone in the past about whom we read. 'Jesus Christ is the same, yesterday, today and for ever,' says the Letter to the Hebrews. Now, I obviously cannot persuade you of that fact. I cannot argue you into accepting it, I do not have to. If Jesus Christ is as alive today as he was then, then he is just as able now as he was then to make himself known to people, to confront them, challenge them to follow him, be rejected by them. In short, everything that happened then still happens. So what you get in the New Testament is not a few pages of history, but a description of what is still happening. He still walks our streets. He still comes in and out of our lives. Here he is still worshipped, there he is still rejected. Still he challenges us, and still his challenge goes unheeded. He crouches still in our doorways, and is raised up on crosses at every street corner. And he still rises from all the deaths we subject him to. The one thing he won't do is go away and leave us alone. He will not let us forget him. Nor will he pressurize us into going to him, though he knows that only then will we find true happiness. He wants us to go to him, of course, but he wants us to *want* to go. He *bids* us, *beseeches* us; he does not command. So it is still easy to avoid him, but only for a time, because one day we shall come to him, either in life or beyond life, and we shall probably all mourn for the time we wasted or looked another way or picked up stones to cast at him.

Jesus is alive, though I have often wished he were not. I have often wished he would go away and leave me alone. But he never does. He still comes to us. The New Testament is about *us*. All life is there. We are all in it. It talks about all the ways we find to deal with this Jesus who stubbornly haunts our history and who will not stay in the grave where they laid him. That is why Christians often go over the story of how they rejected him and nailed him to a cross. It is an old story, to be true, but it is absolutely up to the minute as well. It is true yesterday, today and for ever. All life is there. I am there, and so are you. There are lots of characters in the story as we read it in the New Testament. Some of them have names and some of them do not. Some of them are well known; some of them are unknown, just like us. But all life is there, and all the ways in which men and women react to Jesus.

I want to think first about someone from the story whose name we do not even know, and about whom we know almost nothing. I call him the Secret Admirer. The story of the death of Jesus starts in a private garden, the Garden of Gethsemane. We must not think of it as a public park, like Hyde Park in London or Princes Street Gardens in Edinburgh. It was a private garden, which must have belonged to a wealthy person. He was a secret admirer of Jesus, and he probably put the garden at his disposal: 'Use it any time you like, go there to rest from time to time, try and get away from it all whenever you can.' We don't know how often Jesus did use it, but we do know that he spent his last night on earth there, in torment and foreboding, and it was there that they arrested him in the wee small hours of the morning. Fr Mackay described a visit he made to the Garden of Gethsemane in these words:

> These old olive-trees, if not themselves as old as our Lord's time, may well have sprung as young shoots from the trees he knelt under. The Paschal moon shone through the olive branches as we knelt at our prayers, and threw a confused black and white pattern on the ground. The dogs of the city kept up their distant barking; noises from the streets were carried on the night wind; now and again a trumpet sounded from the citadel, awaking memories of the awful night long ago.

When they came for Jesus, there must have been quite an uproar, and it must have disturbed the sleep of all the well-off people who lived round the garden. But none of them came out to see what was going on. They were too wordly-wise for that. They knew how to keep out of trouble. They knew it was dangerous to meddle, to 'have a go' as they say. So they shoved their heads under their pillows till the noise ceased and Jesus had been taken away. And so did the Secret Admirer. He did not inter-

5

vene. He liked Jesus, admired him, but he did not want to get mixed up in it all.

I have often been a *secret* admirer of Jesus. There has never been a time in my life when I have not known about him, but there have been many times when I have kept him very definitely at a safe distance. I have not wanted to commit myself, make myself look stupid or religious or out of the ordinary. My admiration has often been very secret. Public commitment to Jesus would be more than embarrassing; it might even be painful. So I keep my head well down. I know something important is going on, and I know I am avoiding the challenge. Inside myself I am a little ashamed, because love for Jesus is a difficult thing to keep secret. Nevertheless, I manage to keep it hidden. I am a secret admirer.

2

The Traitor

And immediately, while he was still speaking, Judas came, one of the twelve, and with him a crowd with swords and clubs, from the chief priests and the scribes and the elders. Now the betrayer had given them a sign, saying, 'The one I shall kiss is the man; seize him and lead him away safely.' And when he came, he went up to him at once, and said, 'Master!' And he kissed him. Mark 14:43–5

Judas Iscariot! One of the cruellest riddles of history is to discover why Judas betrayed Jesus. We shall never know exactly, though there are several possible reasons.

There is an old tradition which says that Judas was the nephew of Caiaphas, the high priest who was determined to get rid of Jesus. Judas was persuaded to become a secret agent to plot the downfall of Jesus. Whether this is true or not, it is certainly true that at the end Judas became a tool in the hands of the enemies of our Lord, and he was used to bring about his arrest.

Another explanation is that Judas did it for the money. St John (12:6) tells us that Judas was a thief and had the money box and stole from it. Judas certainly seems to have been the treasurer of our Lord's band of disciples. If he was a thief, as John writing long after maintains, then it is just possible, I suppose, that he betrayed Jesus for a handful of silver.

But neither of these explanations really produces a convincing reason for what he did. The real clue probably lies in his name, 'Iscariot'. This word may be connected with the Latin word 'sicarius', a dagger-bearer, a knifer, a razorman. The Sicarii were fanatical Jewish nationalists, professional revolutionaries, who believed in the violent overthrow of their Roman masters and who promptly disposed of any hapless Jew who got in their way. It is possible that Judas belonged to this company. He probably saw in Jesus the heaven-sent leader, the great charismatic figure who would unite the country against the Roman occupation. There could be two reasons for the betrayal, therefore. When Judas realized that Jesus did not plan to take the way of armed revolt, he could have betrayed him into the hands of his enemies in sheer disgust. This is the kind of thing a disappointed and embittered revolutionary might do. But even more likely is the possibility that Judas tried to force the hand of Jesus by precipitating a crisis. By placing him in a position of danger, he thought he would force Jesus to react violently in his own defence, and the Revolution would be on. It would be the night of the long knives. Blood would flow. The kingdom would be won by violence.

Judas was probably genuinely fond of Jesus, and there are many indications in the gospel that Jesus loved him and had great hopes for him. The kiss need not have been an act of hypocrisy. Maybe Judas saw it as a signal to revolt. 'This is it, Master, the hour is here; buckle on your gun-belt and come.' But, to his horror, Jesus allows himself to be taken. Only this explanation can account for what happens next. Matthew (27:3–5) tells us: 'When Judas, his betrayer, saw that he was condemned, he repented and brought back the thirty pieces of silver to the chief priests and the elders, saying, "I have sinned in betraying innocent blood." They said, "What is that to us? See to it yourself." And throwing down the pieces of silver in the temple, he departed; and he went and hanged himself.' In a moment of devastating insight Judas realizes that he has, in fact, delivered Jesus to death. In that moment he may also have realized the uselessness of the dream on which he had built his whole life: the dream of revolt, of political independence. In total despair he goes and hangs himself, and enters history as the greatest traitor of all time, the man who delivered the Son of God to death. Judas Iscariot.

Judas is not a man with whom we readily identify. We can see ourselves in Peter: those sudden enthusiasms that fade as quickly as they come and leave us more despairing and undisciplined than ever. Or we can see ourselves in Thomas, 'doubting Thomas', the man who wanted his faith constantly fortified by proof. Peter and Thomas, yes. But rarely ever Judas, except in rather rhetorical moments. And yet Judas is probably nearer to our style than these others.

The Christian religion, the Way of Jesus, is costly and painful. It imposes upon us a well-nigh impossible discipline of love: 'By this all men will know that you are my disciples, if you have love for one another' (John 13:35). It is possible to claim to be a follower of Jesus, a member of his Church, and never allow him to challenge our selfishness, our lack of love. Like Judas, we can have Jesus on our own terms. We claim to follow him but, in fact, we try to arrange things so that he follows us or, at least, keeps out of our life.

Judas, in other words, is a person who has his own plans, his own policy, his own style, his own way of doing

9

things, yet who claims that they are Christ's plans, Christ's way of doing things. Christ is always the exclusive possession of our club: he is a revolutionary, if that is what you believe in; or he is a conservative. He belongs to my race and my Church and my group within the Church. Whatever it is you believe in, Christ is on your side, backing up your action, supporting your thing.

We all have fears and prejudices, insecurities and resentments, and we use Christ, not to judge them and heal them and burn them up, but to strengthen and confirm them. We don't really follow Christ. Like Judas, we try to get him to follow us. We try to sign him on. 'Hail Master.' And we betray the Son of Man with a kiss. Judas Iscariot was the man who tried to enlist the Son of God in his private army.

That is why we ought to examine our own record from time to time. We are usually so busy organizing Christ into our own schemes that we never have time to listen to his words and his judgements. That is why we bring all our fear and distrust to the foot of the cross; all our weakness and greed; all our hate and the things that make us bitter. But not these only. Judas's ideas were not all mean. He had a vision of a liberated Palestine and it was a noble vision. But even our noble visions have to be made captive to Christ. We have to bring to him not only our weaknesses to be judged and healed, but our strengths too. All our ideals, all the good causes we give ourselves to, have to be led behind the crucified.

Judas could have been a prince among the apostles if only he had learnt to follow Christ instead of trying to lead him. Alas, I, too, am Judas Iscariot.

3

The Onlooker

And they laid hands on him and seized him. But one of
those who stood by drew his sword, and struck the slave
of the high priest and cut off his ear. And Jesus said to
them, 'Have you come out as against a robber, with
swords and clubs to capture me? Day after day I was with
you in the temple teaching, and you did not seize me. But
let the scriptures be fulfilled.' And they all forsook him,
and fled. And a young man followed him, with nothing
but a linen cloth about his body; and they seized him,
but he left the linen cloth and ran away naked. Mark
14:46–52

St Mark tells us that while Jesus was in the garden with
his disciples, 'Judas, one of the Twelve, appeared, and
with him was a crowd armed with swords and cudgels,
sent by the chief priests, lawyers and elders'. Fr Mackay
describes the scene like this:

The men in the garden were caught in a trap. And
now, in and out among the olives, with swift, unequal
steps, there came the figure of a man – the most terrible
figure in human history. With a quavering 'Hail,
Rabbi!' he did not merely kiss Jesus, but, overdoing
his part, he covered Him with kisses.

As I have already pointed out, the whole episode must

have been disconcerting to the residents of Gethsemane in the adjoining villas. We know that at least one man came out to see what was happening. Our Lord's arrest must have caused quite an uproar. Some of his followers, we are told, tried to make a fight of it, and the high priest's servant had his ear cut off before Jesus calmed things down. One young man, we know for sure, threw on his dressing-gown and ventured into the garden to find out what on earth was happening at such an uncivilized hour. Only St Mark's gospel mentions his presence, in what must be one of the most fascinating footnotes in history. He must have lurked behind an olive tree, watching the strange scene: the exaggerated casualness of Judas; the hysterical violence of the disciples, melting suddenly into fear as they escape through the trees; the neat, professional brutality of the Temple police as they put chains on their prisoner with practised thoroughness; and the powerful and commanding dignity of our Lord at the centre of the scene. All this the young man from the neighbouring villa sees. Then a twig snaps beneath his feet, and the police discover his presence. 'There's another of them! Get hold of him, Jacob!' They lunge after the young man and grab the loose folds of his linen robe. He struggles free and runs away naked, his dressing-gown in the hands of his captors. A footnote to the most momentous night in history: 'He left the linen cloth, and ran away naked.' Rough treatment for a mere onlooker, you may think, yet the Temple police were better theologians than they themselves realized. We are often tempted to be spectators at the Passion, but it is not possible. You have to be on one side or the other. There can be no lurking among the olive trees as detached onlookers. But it is very tempting. Most of us, after all, live close to Gethsemane. We have been brought up in close proximity to Jesus Christ. It is difficult to avoid the knowledge that something is going on. We feel at once fascinated yet repelled, by the strange man in the garden over the wall.

What is it about the Passion of Jesus Christ which so fascinates us, in spite of ourselves, in spite of our desperate attempts not to get too involved? Why are we drawn to the uproar at such odd and defenceless moments? Why can't we just stay indoors and avoid the whole unpleasant business? What are we doing here among these wretched olive trees in this strange half-light, gazing down on that uncomfortably majestic man in chains?

Well, on one level it is because executions fascinate us. You can tell much about a man by the manner of his death. Martyrdom always fascinates lesser men. But what is so special about this martyrdom? There have been others even more dramatic. There have been many men of whom it could be said: 'Nothing in his life became him like the leaving of it.' We know more about the execution of St Thomas More, and about his motives as he went to the block. We can admire the elegant courage of King Charles the Martyr, as he lifts up his long hair to prevent its obstructing the blade of the axe, and there have been countless others who faced death with dignity and courage. Certainly, the courage and dignity of Jesus before his accusers and executioners is compelling, but that alone does not account for the mysterious fascination of the cross. Men have not sung love songs to the guillotine or the hangman's rope. They have not hung small replicas of the electric chair round their necks or clutched them for comfort and reassurance at moments of dread and temptation, and at the moment of death. But all these things have they done to the cross: 'Faithful cross above all other, One and only noble tree.' 'When I survey the

13

wondrous cross.' All this about an instrument of execution! There can be only two reasons for the claims which are made about the crucifixion of Jesus Christ: either they are true; or Christ's death gave rise to the greatest delusion in history, the claim that this event was of cosmic and eternal significance. When you examine what the Church claims was happening, you can no longer remain a spectator. You must commit yourself, either in support of the Church's claims, because you believe they are true; or in opposition to them because you believe they are a massive and paranoid delusion which must be stamped out. You cannot be detached about this man. There can be no hanging back among the olive trees. You are either for or against him.

Tradition tells us that the young man who fled away naked was St Mark himself. He put this little story into his gospel as a sort of signature, a remembrance of the young man who tried to hold back, to look on among the olive trees. That night he fled away naked. But he came back, later, to make his choice and to witness by his own life and death. Am I still holding back? Am I an onlooker at the Passion?

4

The Accuser

And they led Jesus to the high priest; and all the chief
priests and the elders and the scribes were assembled.
. . . The high priest . . . asked Jesus, 'Are you the Christ,
the Son of the Blessed?' And Jesus said, 'I am; and you
will see the Son of man sitting at the right hand of Power,
and coming with the clouds of heaven.' And the high
priest tore his mantle, and said, 'Why do we still need
witnesses? You have heard his blasphemy. What is your
decision?' And they all condemned him as deserving
death. Mark 14:53, 60-4

After they arrested Jesus in the Garden of Gethsemane
they brought him before one of the most powerful men
in Jerusalem to be tried. They brought him face to face
with Caiaphas, the high priest. We do not have high
priests nowadays, and Church courts are not able to sentence anyone to death any longer, but do not make the
mistake of thinking that there are no Caiaphases left.
There is nothing new under the sun. Everything in our
story is still going on. All life is there, and Caiaphas is
still here. He put his finger right on the central problem,
the matter that we have to make up our minds about.
Jesus was sentenced to death for what they called blasphemy: he behaved like God, and he made claims for
himself that no man ever made, claims that implied that

he and God were so close that what he was God was, and what God was he was. No wonder Caiaphas was driven nearly mad with anger and disgust. The story tells us that he tore his robe and said the man had condemned himself with his own words. No other witnesses were needed, because Jesus had, by what he said about himself, pleaded guilty to the charge. And Caiaphas was absolutely right. You cannot just leave a man like Jesus of Nazareth to his own devices. You cannot maintain an attitude of affectionate or even contemptuous neutrality to someone who makes 'himself out to be the Son of God'. You have to make a decision on an issue like that. You must take sides. You must either worship and adore him and give him your life, or condemn him as deserving death. That is the real scandal of Christianity.

The real issue is not the romantic death of an attractive man who was hard done by, but the lifting up upon the cross of one who was both God and Man. How can you be indifferent to a claim like that, a claim that is insane in its absurdity? It is better to be a Caiaphas, better to be an enemy of this man, than a bored and indifferent on-looker. Most people can approve of the ethical teaching of Jesus. Most people can admire the way he faced death. There is little controversy there. That is not what caused the fuss and causes it still. Noble teaching and a noble death do not scandalize people. After a while they simply bore them, and Jesus Christ was not a bore. He was either insane or he was the incarnate Son of God, and you must take sides on that one. He demands your total allegiance or your total opposition. They didn't crucify Jesus because of his politics, contrary to what many theologians claim, or simply because he was a good man and most other men in Jerusalem were evil, contrary to the claim of some preachers. They crucified him because he claimed to be the Son of God. The charge was quite specific: blasphemy of a sort that no Jew could tolerate; sacrilege of unbelievably momentous proportions. This man claimed to be God among men. He told the Jews that they could cease their Temple worship for a while, since the object of their worship was among them. Imagine if a man burst into your church during the service on Easter Day and shouted, 'Don't go to the altar, don't make your communion. You don't have to receive me under the forms of bread and wine, because I am here in your midst in the flesh. The shadow has departed, the reality has come. I am among you.' Since men have grown more tender, and blasphemy bothers us little today, we would simply have him committed to a mental hospital. The Jew took these things much more seriously. The penalty for this enormous blasphemy was death. To the Jew the issue was simple. You either fall down and worship this man, or you hang him on a tree. Detachment wasn't possible, nor is it possible today. You see, if what this man said of himself is true, then it concerns you whether you like it or not. You cannot escape from it.

Nowadays, we have various ways round this challenge. We say that they crucified Jesus because of his politics. Well, that is just not true. It is true that they used a political argument to get the Romans to execute him, because that was the only way to achieve their purpose. (The irony is that on the very day they killed Jesus, they released a real terrorist called Barabbas in order to please the Jerusalem mob, but Jesus they delivered up to death.) Nor is it true that they killed him because he was a good man and all the other important Jews were evil. That is a terrible lie, and it has darkened the very face of history and given rise to the most evil form of racism known to man: anti-Semitism. They crucified Jesus for blasphemy, for making a claim about himself that most sane men would find unacceptable. Nowadays, of course, we wouldn't execute such a man. This is the point made by Studdert Kennedy. At Golgotha, he says, men at least crucified Christ, they responded to him with passion and strength, but

> When Jesus came to Birmingham they simply passed him by,
> They never hurt a hair of him, they simply let him die;
> For men had grown more tender, and they would not give him pain,
> They only just passed down the street, and left him in the rain.
>
> Still Jesus cried, 'Forgive them, for they know not what they do',
> And still it rained the wintry rain that drenched him through and through;
> The crowds went home and left the streets without a soul to see,
> And Jesus crouched against a wall and cried for Calvary.

What Caiaphas did was better, much better. You must either fall down and worship this man or fight him to death. You must respond with passion. Who can hold the unbelievable facts in their mind, and remain unaffected? Even as I recite them they thrill and scandalize me: the everlasting Father among us in Christ, a trembling foetus in the womb of Mary; God among us, in the dust and tears of Galilee; God among us in the streets of Jerusalem, in the olive groves of Gethsemane. God among us, raised high on a cross. Who can be indifferent to these claims? Not Caiaphas, certainly; certainly not he. But what about me? Will I stand back for ever?

5

The Deserter

And after a little while again the bystanders said to Peter, 'Certainly you are one of them; for you are a Galilean.' But he began to invoke a curse on himself and to swear, 'I do not know this man of whom you speak.' And immediately the cock crowed a second time. And Peter remembered how Jesus had said to him, 'Before the cock crows twice, you will deny me three times.' And he broke down and wept. Mark 14:70–2

All life is there. In the story of the suffering and the death of Christ there are all sorts of characters. We call them bit parts or walk-on actors, who appear briefly, perform their part in the drama, and disappear without further mention. We never even learn their names. But there are others with more important parts, central actors in the unfolding events: Jesus himself, Judas, a name dark with guilt and shame, and Caiaphas, the vehement and articulate high priest who brought about his death. And there is Peter. Next to Jesus, it is Peter I love best, Peter with whom I identify. Peter the deserter, the boastful and impulsive; Peter the leader; Peter the man who denied his master. His part in the story is the most heart-breaking, and I cannot read it without a lump in my throat. After the arrest in the garden, Peter followed on at a safe distance. During the trial he stood outside in the court-yard warming himself at a fire burning in a brazier during the chill hours before dawn. There he was challenged three times by some of the onlookers and servants: 'Surely you are one of his followers?' Each time Peter denied it with an oath: 'I do not know this man.' After the third denial the cock crowed twice, signalling the end of that tormented night in the strange half-light before the break of day. Peter, we read, remembered the words of Jesus: 'Before the cock crows twice, you will deny me three times.' And he broke down and wept.

How well I know that feeling, how often I have tasted those tears of terrible regret after my own many denials of Jesus. That is why I love Peter. I love him because he was a failure, a deserter, a terribly human man who found that following Jesus was almost impossibly difficult. Peter was no hero. He was not one of those superhuman perfect Christians who make you shiver in your shoes as you contemplate their achievements, their holiness, their up-rightness. We all know people like that; they make us feel judged and found wanting, consigned to the ranks of the second-class. But not Peter. Peter, like most of us, did not make a very good Christian, and the New Testament does not try to pretend otherwise. That is why it is such a marvellous book to read, with its failures and betrayals, its tears and its great sorrows. And the tale of failure again and again features Peter.

Peter wasn't his real name. His real name was Simon. Peter was a nickname which meant rock! Jesus gave him the nickname, and it does not seem very apt, does it, for someone who crumbled again and again? Maybe there was some humour in the name. But it was just as likely that Jesus saw something in Peter that would finally, after many failures, become firm and constant, like rock. But it took a long time, a very long time. All through his life Peter was constantly failing, making a mess of things, betraying those whom he loved. He failed Christ in little things, just like us. But we fail him in the big things too, or would, if we were put to the test. Peter did. Even at a moment of supreme danger and threat to the one he loved most of all in the world, he failed. Peter misunderstood much about Jesus, and made many mistakes in trying to change Jesus into someone more acceptable to him and to others. But there was one thing he really understood about his Lord: he knew that Jesus was one who forgave sins, and not only once or twice, but *always*. That one thing he learnt, and it meant that Peter was able to keep on and on, after failure. In spite of all his weaknesses, Peter was great in one thing: he never, finally, gave up. He fell at all the fences, but he just picked himself up and struggled on, blinded with tears and covered with mire. And that was his glory. It was this quality which Jesus must have detected in him, this refusal ever to accept defeat. In his long life Peter lost all the battles, but he finally won the war.

There is a lovely tradition which says that Peter was in Rome when the Emperor Nero started a savage persecution of the Church. Rome was in flames, and Peter started walking away from the terror. He set out along the Appian Way, an old man now, weary from all his journeyings for Christ, not sure what he ought to do or where he ought to go. And as he trudged away from Rome, Jesus met him, going back in the direction of the city. Peter asked him the famous question: 'Quo vadis, Domine?' 'Where are you going, Lord?' 'I go to Rome to die for you,' replied Jesus. Peter, we are told, stopped and turned round slowly, and this time he did not fail: he went back to Rome and death.

People like us can learn a good deal from Peter. His real secret was humility. It takes humility to struggle on in spite of repeated failure. Only the proud and self-pitying are defeated by failure. The humble man, however, soon shakes off the failures of the past. He never had an inflated idea of himself in the first place. He knows that he will not be judged by his successes but by his perseverance, so he picks himself up, swallows the lump in his throat, and struggles on. That was Peter's way. When they came to crucify him, he asked to be crucified upside down, because he felt unworthy to die in the same position as his Lord. If you, like me, are not much of a Christian, then Peter's story will give you courage. No matter what your failures are, pick yourself up and, even if tears are blinding you, do not give up the struggle.

6

The Politician

So when Pilate saw that he was gaining nothing, but rather that a riot was beginning, he took water and washed his hands before the crowd, saying, 'I am innocent of this righteous man's blood; see to it yourselves.' And all the people answered, 'His blood be on us and on our children!' Then he released for them Barabbas, and having scourged Jesus, delivered him to be crucified. Matthew 27:24–6

In *The Man Born to be King*, Dorothy L. Sayers describes the dream Claudia Procla, the wife of Pontius Pilate, had:

PILATE: Claudia, Claudia, tell me what was this dream of yours?

CLAUDIA: I was in a ship at sea, voyaging among the islands of the Aegean. At first the weather seemed calm and sunny but presently, the sky darkened, and the sea began to toss with the wind . . . Then out of the east, there came a cry, strange and piercing. 'Pan ho megas tethneke. Pan ho megas tethneke.' . . . And I said to the captain, 'What do they cry?' And he answered, 'Great Pan is dead.' And I asked him, 'How can God die?' And he answered, 'Don't you remem-

ber? They crucified him. He suffered under
Pontius Pilate.' . . . Then all the people in
the ship turned their faces to me and said:
'Pontius Pilate . . . Pontius Pilate. He suffered under Pontius Pilate . . . crucified,
dead and buried . . . sub Pontio Pilato
. . . Pilate . . . he suffered . . . suffered
. . . under Pontius Pilate . . . under Pontius
Pilate . . .' in all tongues and all voices
. . . even the little children with their mothers . . . suffered under Pontio Pilato . . .
crucifié sous Ponce-Pilate . . . gekreuzigt
unter Pontius Pilatus' . . . your name, husband, your name continually, 'he suffered
under Pontius Pilate'.

Claudia Procla heard her husband's name sounding
through the centuries. And, of course, it has. The Christ-
ian creeds have carried the message down the ages: 'Jesus
Christ his only Son our Lord . . . suffered under Pontius
Pilate, was crucified, dead and buried.' 'One Lord Jesus
Christ . . . was crucified also for us under Pontius Pilate.
He suffered and was buried.' Pontius Pilate. Why is he
in the creed?

Well, the obvious answer, though not the really important one, is that the use of his name firmly fixes the
crucifixion in history. We are dealing here with an event
as definite as today's headlines. He was crucified under
Pontius Pilate. Pontius Pilate was governor of Judaea
from AD 26 to AD 36, when he was recalled to Rome. We
know a fair bit about him. He showed very little under-
standing of the Jews whom he was sent to govern, though,
to be fair, few Romans would have known how to deal
with a people as obsessed with religion as were the Jews.

Early on in his term of office he caused a violent disturbance by using Temple funds to build an aqueduct. And there is evidence that on two or three occasions he was ruthless in suppressing religious violence. But one can sympathize with him. Religious bitterness is very difficult to deal with. The nearest modern parallel I can draw is this: imagine a fastidiously agnostic Oxford don sent to govern Northern Ireland, seething with religious tension. Can you imagine his frustration and disdain and final cynicism as he picks his way through confrontations with the IRA and UDA? No, Pontius Pilate had a difficult job to do, and it is to his credit that he stuck it for ten years.

Towards the end of his stay in Judaea he gave permission for the execution of Jesus of Nazareth. It happened about AD 33. Pontius Pilate and his wife were both impressed by Jesus, and Pilate did try to release him, but by this time he was a cynical and probably very tired man. So, we read, he handed Jesus over to be crucified.

We do not know what happened to Pontius Pilate after that. He steps out of history, though legends abound. One has it that he later became a Christian, and the Abyssinian Church has canonized him. Another legend has it that, like Judas, he later committed suicide. There are legends about his wife too. The Greek Church canonized her. We cannot be certain of these things. All we know is that during his term of office as governor of Judaea he crucified Jesus. And his name has been a date stamp on the Christian creed ever since.

But there is another reason why Pontius Pilate is in the creed and this reason is more important and more complex. To explain it I want to digress for a moment. Most of us have been brought up on the good guys versus the bad guys theory of history. In fact, history and human nature are much more complicated than that. I want to give you an example from politics to illustrate this. My example is about Churchill. A few years ago I saw the controversial play by the German playwright, Rolf Hochhuth, called *Soldiers*. In this play Hochhuth tried to prove that Churchill was a war criminal. Apart altogether from that, the play raises a fascinating and insoluble human dilemma. Churchill went to war to defeat the hideous spectre of Hitler's Germany. You will remember that it was Hitler's invasion of Poland that brought Britain into the war. Towards the end of the war things are still in the balance and Churchill is in an appalling dilemma. He cannot beat Germany without Russia's help, and Stalin's Russia is as great an evil as Hitler's Germany. In order to make certain that Russia will not make an independent arrangement with Germany, he has to turn a blind eye to Russia's occupation of the East European countries, including Poland. It is expedient that Poland be sacrificed to Russia rather than that the whole of Europe perish. Here we see the anguish of the man in power. What he did was wrong. He sacrificed Poland and all those Eastern European lands to communist domination in order to save the rest of Europe from a Hitler–Stalin pact. What would we have done in his place?

The affairs of men rarely allow for a simple choice between good and evil, light and darkness. Whatever you choose to do is wrong because the whole of our nature is wrong; there is a profound distortion at the root of things which makes all our choices corrupt to some degree. And this was Pilate's dilemma. He was in an appalling situation. If he released Jesus he would provoke a riot, many would be killed and reports would be sent to Rome. His own usefulness in a tense situation would be compromised. On the other hand Jesus is innocent, and he knows it, and the whole genius of Roman law was, in theory, for the protection of a man's rights. How was he to act? Jesus, we read, recognized his dilemma and had compassion on him, compassion because he was in a position of power. 'You would have no power over me, unless it had been given you from above; therefore he who delivered me to you has the greater sin' (John 19:11). The Christian by this word is called upon to feel compassion for those in power; to sympathize with them in their dilemmas.

Pilate made the inevitable decision, the only decision he could make. He sacrificed one innocent man for the sake of maintaining peace. Churchill and Poland. Pilate and Christ. What other decision was humanly possible? We would have done the same. And yet, we know both decisions were wrong. What is this tragic flaw in humanity that forces us to these decisions? And we have all made decisions like this. We have turned our backs on the needs of others, on the demands they make on us, because we have other responsibilities. We have families, we have jobs, we have unavoidable obligations. We live in the midst of excruciating dilemmas. *I* am Pontius Pilate. Every day I make the unavoidable decision to hand over Christ. He suffered under Pontius Pilate. I am Pontius Pilate, and he allows himself to suffer at my hands. These are some of the most momentous words in history. God loves us and pities our dilemmas. He has compassion upon our impossible predicaments. He stretches out towards us just as we are: soiled with compromises, heavy with the burden of wrong decisions, laden with greater and lesser infidelities. He does not hold back till I make the right decisions, till I purify myself. He comes to me, recognizing my unavoidable sinfulness and accepts me in spite of it. And the cross is the demonstration of this incredible love. He does not judge us and condemn us in

27

our dilemmas. He himself becomes the victim of our dilemmas. He bears them in his own body on the tree.

He suffered under Pontius Pilate. I am Pontius Pilate. *I* am in the creed, because my Lord allows himself to suffer at my hands. He knows my dilemmas and my weaknesses, and he takes them upon himself. And as I lay the cross upon his back he gazes at me, with compassion. Because, you see, I am Pontius Pilate.

7

The Executioner

And when they came to a place called Golgotha (which means the place of a skull), they offered him wine to drink, mingled with gall; but when he tasted it, he would not drink it. And when they had crucified him, they divided his garments among them by casting lots; then they sat down and kept watch over him there. Matthew 27:33–6

Caiaphas and Pontius Pilate were responsible for the death of Jesus, but they didn't, of course, do the dirty work themselves. The Caiaphases and Pilates of this world never do. They may be the men that declare the wars, but they are never the ones that do the fighting or the dying. There are always others, plenty of others, to do the dirty work for them. It is always someone else who hammers in the nails or pushes in the bayonet; it is always the man under orders.

We don't know anything about the executioners who laid Jesus on the cross and stretched out his arms and prized open his fingers, before they drove the thick nails through the thin flesh on to the beam behind. They had nothing against him, of course, and probably had never even heard of him. But they would not, in any case, look him in the eyes. Their job concentrated on his hands and his feet. You had to forget their faces to get through the job at all. 'Never look them in the face,' the older executioners would tell the younger, 'or you'll never get the job done.' *His* eyes were certainly to be avoided. His eyes were great and dark with love, and to get on with the job at all you had to ignore them, turn away from them, put on a gruffness and a toughness you didn't feel. Usually the victims cursed and swore and fought like tigers, and it took several men to hold them down. This one was different. You sensed, not fear or hatred, but a terrible sorrow in him, an ancient longing which made everything seem strangely muffled and distant. It was as though this thing which was happening, this thing you were doing with that rough hammer and those cruel nails was happening somewhere else. Sure enough, it was happening here and now on this Friday morning, but it seemed to be happening somewhere else too, somewhere beyond time. It was the strangest thing. It was as if a great door shut suddenly somewhere back beyond time and a cry pierced you as if God wept. And then you heard him praying: 'Father, forgive them; for they know not what they do.' Then you all grabbed the cross and lifted it into its socket up there on the hill, and that door shut again, and again that cry was heard somewhere else out of time. Hastily, you picked up your tools and walked away, and you could not bear to turn round and look at him till you were far enough away not to see his eyes. It took two jugs of wine before you stopped shivering.

History is full of them, but we know none of their names. They are the men under orders, the men doing a job, a filthy job, a job they must do to keep their families fed, to pay the rent. They are the ones who build the gallows and make them strong. Other men send the victims. They are the men who make sure the train to the concentration camp leaves on time. Other men send the passengers. They are the men who service the gas ovens. Other men sign the papers that send in the women and children. They have a job to do, and because they do it, because they obey orders without fuss, every tyranny in history has been built on their compliance, their reliance on wages.

But we dare not condemn them because we, too, are the executioners. We are all enclosed in this web of guilt in great ways and small. I depend for my material need upon men who work underground to dig my coal. I put out my garbage on the pavement and another man must lift it, tons of it, to keep my street tidy. It is in my name that young men with guns are parading the streets of Northern Ireland. My fondness for tea and coffee means back-breaking labour and low wages for thousands of peasants. We are all part of one another, and somewhere another man's pain is caused by my pleasure. Mine are the hands that wield the mallet that bangs in the nails, not another's. And there is no way out of this web, this maze of guilt and responsibility for one another. It is an inescapable part of being human. We exploit and degrade one another in ways we do not even know. We are all part of one another, and we are all, in some sense, guilty of one another's miseries. There is no way we can creep out from under this guilt, once we recognize it.

This is why the cross of Jesus is for us an object both of sorrow and of joy: sorrow, because this is what we do day after day, joy, because at the very moment we bang in the nails he forgives us. No matter how hard we try, we cannot kill God's love for us. He forgives and forgives and forgives. And there is no more terrible word in any language than that, once you feel its meaning and its cost. There is no weapon effective against that unwearying

31

love. There is nothing we can do against it. That is why one day, after all our striving and folly and flight, we will go to him, defeated, conquered by the strange victim we thought we had done with. His cross will have the victory. His love will win. He knew it. It cost him dear, but he knew it. That is why he said: 'I, when I am lifted up from the earth, will draw all men to myself' (John 12:32).

PART II

THE WORDS

1

The First Word

And when they came to the place which is called The Skull, there they crucified him, and the criminals, one on the right and one on the left. And Jesus said, 'Father, forgive them; for they know not what they do.' Luke 23:33–4

According to the evangelists, Matthew, Mark, Luke and John, our Lord uttered seven sayings, seven 'words', on the cross during the six hours he hung there from nine in the morning till three in the afternoon. The traditional arrangement is that he uttered the first three words between the hours of nine in the morning and noon; and the other four between noon and three o'clock when he died.

Luke and John each record three words, and the fourth and central saying is contained in Matthew and in Mark. There's nothing strange about this apparently arbitrary distribution of sayings between the four evangelists, because most of the traditions about our Lord were picked up and put down by them as they had occasion, and we know that there were various groups of listeners on the sacred mount where they crucified him. We know that the apostles forsook him, but we are also told that Peter followed afar off later on. He must have been lurking somewhere in the background, in the outer ring of scoffing bystanders. Mark tells us, 'And they led Jesus to the high priest; and all the chief priests and the elders and the scribes were assembled. And Peter had followed him at a distance' (14:54).

We can be quite certain that he wasn't the only one of the disciples who had deserted him after the arrest, who followed at a distance. Some had the courage to come close: our Lady and the beloved apostle John were at the foot of the cross, and there were other women there, too. When we come to the third word, we shall note that there were four women clustered around the foot of the cross.

Incidentally, it is worth meditating on the role of women in the Passion of our Lord. Unlike the men around him, they showed courage and devotion, a courage and devotion which have frequently characterized Christian women, very often in the face of the cowardice of Christian men. The women who followed our Lord never seem to have failed him. They followed him to the end, when their more aggressive brothers had deserted him.

We must think, therefore, of various groups of bystanders around the cross, some a little on one side, some a little on the other; and we must think of our Lord raised only about eighteen inches above the bystanders. We tend to have an exalted view, a kind of Metro-Goldwyn-Mayer view, of the crucifixion. Maybe we see it in a rosy light, our Lord beautifully made-up, on an exquisitely carved crucifix, high above calvary, like a reredos high above a cathedral altar. This was not the case. Since the crucified was only slightly above the people who were standing around the foot of the cross, they could very easily hear what he said.

But before we meditate on the first word, let us run over the events which preceded it.

Our Lord was arrested in the Garden of Gethsemane in the middle of the night, and went through six trials in the hours that followed, before he was finally led out to the place of execution. Before he bore the cross, he was scourged. Scourging was itself almost a form of capital punishment. It was hideously effective. The victim was tied to a pillar and stripped. His back was flayed with a whip in which were pieces of bone or steel or iron which literally laid the man's back open. As one theologian has described it, 'Scourging always preceded crucifixion, reducing the naked body to strips of raw flesh, and inflamed and bleeding weals, and when afterwards the victim's hands were nailed to the cross-piece and his feet tied to the base of the beam, nothing could have been more horrible or appalling.'

Our Lord endured all this. Then he was given the cross-beam and made to walk to the Mount of Calvary. He stumbled two or three times, and we know that Simon of Cyrene was made to bear part of the cross. St Mark tells us, in one of those interesting little footnotes of his, that Simon was the father of Alexander and Rufus. What depth of devotion and private history may lie behind this footnote! This man was plucked out of the crowd and was pressed into helping Our Lord to bear the cross-beam. Simon and his sons, Alexander and Rufus, must have been known to Mark's readers as Christians, perhaps in Rome, so straightforwardly are the names introduced. If we could peel the layers off this incident, we might discover that Simon and his sons became Christians as a result of this strange and tragic encounter, and passed the story on to Mark. These are the kind of tantalizing details in the gospels which never tell us enough. We only know that Simon of Cyrene saw the poor man of Nazareth lying in the dust of a Jerusalem street, and helped him to carry his cross.

When they arrived on the hill the victims were stripped naked and thrown down on the rude beams. At this point there was usually an enormous struggle. The victims would curse and swear and fight with their executioners. The contrast between the behaviour of the criminals and our Lord was both poignant and bitter. Luke tells us that as they nailed our Lord to the cross he said, 'Father, forgive them, for they know not what they do.'

Forgive whom? The Romans, certainly, the soldiers and the impersonal executioners, as well as Pilate, with his busy, officious desire to keep the peace in that turbulent city. And the Jews as well, who had called for his death and delivered him to Pilate to be crucified. But behind the Romans and Jews there presses the whole of mankind. Just as the city where they crucified our Lord is every city, so are his executioners all of us. The first word, then, is a word of forgiveness, and it is spoken to us who take part, in many different ways, in the crucifixion of our Lord. Part of our sin is a kind of ignorance. We know not, most of the time, what we do. Paul, in the First Letter to the Corinthians, said, 'None of the rulers of this age understood this; for if they had, they would not have crucified the Lord of glory' (1 Cor 2:8). They did not know who he was. In the great parable of judgement in Matthew, chapter 25, those who are standing before our Lord all plead ignorance: 'When did we see thee hungry or thirsty . . . or naked . . . or in prison?' And he answers, 'As you did it not to one of the least of these, you did it not to me.' We did not know that God was in all the challenges that came before us and our compassion. We did not know who was hurt by our sins. So, in a sense, we sin against ourselves ignorantly.

38

Do you remember our Lord's lament over the city of Jerusalem when he saw it as he was coming into it for the last time? He stopped there and gazed down upon it from the brow of the hill, and he looked at it, shining white in the heat: 'Jerusalem, Jerusalem.' And he wept over it, we are told, because it did not know the things that belonged unto its peace. If only it had known he was sent to it! If only it had known that he wanted to gather all Jerusalem and its citizens in his arms as a hen gathers its chickens, and they would not! So we feel all the pain and patience and pity of God for us for the ignorant ways in which we have denied his approach to us.

Yet, in some sense, we *do* know what we do, because there is often a wilfulness about our sinning, about our selfishness. We deliberately, perversely sabotage our own joy. And we have done it so often. We have done things we know will cause us, afterwards, to burn with remorse. So, as we meditate upon this word, we must think of our ignorant sins *and* our wilful sins, our crying sins and our secret sins. We must pray the prayer Eric Milner White adapted from John Donne:

Forgive me, O Lord
O Lord forgive me my sins,
    the sins of my youth,
    the sins of the present;
    the sins I laid upon myself in an ill pleasure,
    the sins I cast upon others in an ill example;
    the sins which are manifest to all the world,
    the sins which I have laboured to hide from mine
        acquaintance,
      from my own conscience,
      and even from my memory;

my crying sins and my whispering sins,
my ignorant sins and my wilful;
sins against my superiors, equals, servants, against
my lovers and benefactors,
sins against myself, mine own body, my own soul;
sins against thee, O almighty Father, O merciful Son,
O blessed Spirit of God.

All this we must meditate upon, because this scene at the very beginning of the last act of our Lord's life imposes a most intolerable truth upon us. He forgives us. He gives back to us all the pain and despite we have done to him. He is bruised and butchered by our sins, and he forgives us. This really is the heart of the Christian Gospel, and it is intolerable because most of us do not want to be forgiven. We want somehow to make up for our wrongdoing, or we want to be punished for it; we want to earn forgiveness. We want to feel a smouldering, gnawing kind of guilt, but he will not permit it. He suffers what we do, that we may amend freely. How can we carry on one moment longer in iniquity when we see what it does to him and how he bears it?

This is the heart of the Christian Gospel. The cross is a placard, an advertisement, showing us the consequences to God of our activities. There is a very poignant bit in Helen Waddell's novel about Peter Abelard which captures this:

He pointed to a fallen tree beside them, sawn through the middle. 'That dark ring there, it goes up and down the whole length of the tree. But you only see it where it is cut across. That is what Christ's life was; the bit of God that we saw. And we think God is like that, because Christ was like that, kind, and forgiving sins and healing people. We think God is like that for ever, because it happened once, with Christ. But not the pain. Not the agony at the last. We think that stopped.'

Abelard looked at him, the blunt nose and the wide mouth, the honest troubled eyes. He could have knelt before him. 'Then, Thibault,' he said slowly, 'you think that all this,' he looked down at the little quiet body in his arms, 'all the pain of the world was Christ's cross?' 'God's cross,' said Thibault. 'And it goes on.'

There can only be two responses to that intolerable word of forgiveness. The first is to accept the forgiveness. Identify in you what hammers in the nails. Do not shirk that act of self-examination. Know the worst against yourself, and then receive the forgiveness that is freely offered. But as you gaze upon that placard, that advertisement of the eternal pain, passion and forgiveness of God, make amendment, for how can you bear to let it go on one moment longer? That forgiving pain of God must have an end sometime. Make amendment, so that henceforth you will not be one who drives the nails into our Lord, but one who, with him, heals the pain and shares the burden.

2

The Second Word

One of the criminals who were hanged railed at him,
saying, 'Are you not the Christ? Save yourself and us!'
But the other rebuked him, saying, 'Do you not fear God,
since you are under the same sentence of condemnation?
And we indeed justly; for we are receiving the due reward
of our deeds; but this man has done nothing wrong.' And
he said, 'Jesus, remember me when you come in your
kingly power.' And he said to him, 'Truly, I say to you,
today you will be with me in Paradise.' Luke 23:39–43

The two criminals heard and saw everything that happened to our Lord on the Mount of Calvary, and one of
them joined in the railing. It is a strange fact that victims
often cooperate with their persecutors in crimes against
other victims. It is one of the strangest elements of human
perversity, that there are always some among the weak
who will join with the strong in oppressing the weak. All
those who in history and in daily life join their oppressors
debase themselves in the face of their own tormentors. Is
there a grosser, more demeaning spectacle in history than
the sight of this coarse and brutal criminal in his own
death throes, turning his head to join with the rabble who
have put him up where he is, in taunting his fellow victim?
The weak who join the bully in persecution: have we
done it, perhaps? Have we, in order to avoid drawing

attention to our own weakness, joined with the strong in pursuing other weak people?

Certainly Peter did something like this during that awful night. We must remember poor Peter, who was lying back in the shadows of this night.

> Now Peter was sitting outside in the courtyard. And a maid came up to him, and said, 'You also were with Jesus the Galilean.' But he denied it before them all, saying, 'I do not know what you mean.' And when he went out to the porch, another maid saw him, and she said to the bystanders, 'This man was with Jesus of Nazareth.' And again he denied it with an oath, 'I do not know the man.' After a little while the bystanders came up and said to Peter, 'Certainly you are also one of them, for your accent betrays you.' Then he began to invoke a curse on himself and to swear, 'I do not know the man.' And immediately the cock crowed. And Peter remembered the saying of Jesus. 'Before the cock crows, you will deny me three times.' And he went out and wept bitterly.   Matthew 26:69–75

The weak turn against themselves. They are miracles of perversity. But there is another miracle at that moment on the hill where they crucified him: the miracle of awareness. Maybe the penitent thief had heard Jesus during the two or three years of his ministry. Maybe he knew someone who had been healed by him. Maybe his sister or his brother had followed Jesus and had seen the mighty works that he did, and had heard the searching words that he spoke and had seen his tenderness and his care for the weak. We do not know. Certainly, it would have been difficult not to have heard something about Jesus. Maybe this thief had been mildly intrigued by our Lord. But he was tough. It is a strange thing, this toughness, isn't it, which is really a kind of weakness? I know a little bit about this because I went to a tough school and was a tough kid. Yet, God called me to be a priest, and I was acutely embarrassed! I remember how I was unable to tell the boys I was with why I was leaving Scotland to go to a foreign country south of the border. They could not understand what was happening to me. I could not tell them I was going to be a priest. It was a weak kind of thing to be. And this kind of weakness, which vests itself in a swaggering, macho kind of toughness, is really evidence of a feeble inner life, or no inner life at all.

Maybe the penitent thief was like this. He was a man's man, who never really thought below the surface of life until at this moment he was brought to a moment of truth and realization. There are two elements in this. The first is obviously his own death. The thought of one's own death, as Dr Johnson reminded us, marvellously concentrates the mind. All temporal and transitory considerations were cut away. There was nothing left for him among those former friends. The world held nothing, and he gazed into his own death, and death was the prelude to revelation. It still is. It cuts through the chatter and noise and distraction of our mind, and makes us mind the things that matter. 'Memento mori,' the ancients used to say, 'remember to die, remember you are this day on the way to death.' And what is it that matters to you at that point? We must all of us find these moments to concentrate on the certainty that there will one day be an end, maybe sooner than we think. The man on the cross came to that moment, that prelude to revelation which the certainty of his own death meant.

Then he did another thing: he really looked at Jesus for the first time, and he was suddenly overwhelmed. He looks and looks hard, and everything else is blotted out as he sees the majesty, the humility, and the strength of the man. The eyes of Christ hold him. He looks at Christ, and he has a moment of revelation. At last he recognizes the truth. We must do the same. If we would find Jesus, we must look steadily at him. If we would know and be freed by the truth, we must learn to look at Jesus, maybe for the first time. We do not give ourselves a chance otherwise. Look to Jesus, fix your eyes upon him. The criminal did, and then he made his clumsy, uneducated act of faith. His mind was a jumble of messianic notions, political revolution and spiritual longings. He turns to the majestic, yet wounded figure beside him and says, 'When you come into your kingdom, remember me.' And the response of Jesus is momentous and comforting, 'Truly, I say to you, today you will be with me in paradise.'

The word 'paradise' comes from the Persian, as a loan word to the Greek, meaning an enclosed park or pleasure garden. The original Greek translation of the Old Testament used it for the Garden of Eden, and then it was developed as a superterrestial place of blessedness, a paradise, the place where God was. The word is only used twice elsewhere in the New Testament. In 2 Corinthians Paul describes one of his own mystical experiences: 'And I know that this man was caught up into Paradise – whether in the body or out of the body I do not know, God knows' (2 Corinthians 12:3). Paul was caught up out of the body and given a glimpse of heaven. And we find the word again in the Book of Revelation: 'He who has an ear, let him hear what the Spirit says to the churches. To him who conquers I will grant to eat of the tree of life, which is in the paradise of God' (Revelation 2:7).

Our Lord assured the penitent that that very day he would be with him after death with God in heaven. It is pointless to speculate or try to be specific about the precise order or levels of God's presence, or get into theological disputes about the nature of paradise, or whether there are grades in it, or whether we really deserve to enter it. All that matters is that our Lord promised a life after death: 'Today you will be with me in paradise.' It is important to understand the depth and scope of this promise, because our Lord knew of what he spoke. He came from the Father. 'He came down from heaven', as our creed says, and he assured us of eternal life. This is one of the most important elements of his teaching.

> Jesus said to her, 'I am the resurrection and the life; he who believes in me, though he die, yet shall he live, and whoever lives and believes in me shall never die. Do you believe this?' (John 11:25–6).
>
> 'Let not your hearts be troubled; believe in God, believe also in me. In my Father's house are many rooms; if it were not so, would I have told you that I go to prepare a place for you? And when I go and prepare a place for you, I will come again and will take you to myself, that where I am you may be also. And you know the way where I am going.' (John 14:1–4).

The Christian faith is based on a solid conviction of the life of the world to come. Paul says, 'If for this life only we have hoped in Christ, we are of all men most to be pitied' (1 Cor 15:19). Christ came to forgive and sanctify us. He came to teach us about the true nature of God. And he came to assure us of life after death. If you remove this third element, the other two are beside the point. What good to me is a God who forgives, if I become nothing at death? What good will my knowledge of the reality of God be, if I have only this life in which to meditate upon it? By this word we are enabled to receive that promise into our hearts, and let it strengthen us for the great struggle of our Christian life. We have the whole of eternity to aspire to, to long for. With that knowledge, we are not separated from those we love. We are not bereft, but following after those we 'have loved long since and lost a while', in Newman's great phrase. And we are not bereft even of those we have never known in the flesh. Have you never felt close to the great heroes and saints as you have read their words and meditated upon their lives? We are not separated from them. I have often felt them beside me.

Nothing can ultimately separate us from the love of God, and those who are separated from us by death. So this word asks us to do two things: it asks us to look at Jesus, maybe for the first time. Look away from all else. Look only unto him. And then it asks us to look through Jesus into eternity, to the great homeland that awaits us, the land of the Trinity, deep heaven, a place prepared for us by our blessed Lord.

3

The Third Word

When the soldiers had crucified Jesus they took his garments and made four parts, one for each soldier. . . . But
the tunic was without seam, woven from top to bottom;
so they said to one another, 'Let us not tear it, but cast
lots for it to see whose it shall be.' . . . So the soldiers
did this. But standing by the cross of Jesus were his
mother, and his mother's sister, Mary the wife of Clopas,
and Mary Magdalene. When Jesus saw his mother, and
the disciple whom he loved standing near, he said to his
mother, 'Woman, behold, your son!' Then he said to the
disciple, 'Behold, your mother!' And from that hour the
disciple took her to his own home. John 19:23–7

We must understand, although there is some ambiguity,
that there were four women standing with John at the
foot of the cross. John writes, 'Standing by the cross of
Jesus were his mother, and his mother's sister.' And then
he goes on, 'Mary, the wife of Clopas.' This refers to a
third person. We know from other sources that our Lady's
sister was Salome, and she was the mother of James and
John, the sons of Zebedee. So she was the mother of the
beloved disciple who was standing there. Mary, the wife
of Clopas, is listed after our Lady's sister. Clopas was
perhaps the brother of St Joseph, our Lord's foster-
father. The fourth in the group was Mary Magdalene,

who owed so much to our Lord. John never mentions his own name, or the name of any member of his family, in the book he wrote. He is almost completely self-effacing, lying back in the shadows. He talks about 'the mother of Jesus and his mother's sister', never about 'my mother, Salome, the wife of Zebedee'. In the same way he only refers to himself as 'the disciple whom Jesus loved'.

So we must understand that there are four women grouped around the foot of the cross, balancing the four soldiers on the other side, who had stripped Jesus of his clothes. This immediately strikes a particularly poignant note. Almost certainly these women who provided for our Lord and his band of apostles, were the ones who had made the very garments which the soldiers greedily and callously divided among themselves.

> And the twelve were with him, and also some women who had been healed of evil spirits and infirmities: Mary, called Magdalene, from whom seven demons had gone out, and Joanna, the wife of Chuza, Herod's steward, and Susanna, and many others, who provided for them out of their means. Luke 8:1–3

The four women watched the four hardened and un-affected soldiers pulling off these clothes and dividing them up. One grabs the seamless robe or tunic, which was the under-garment worn next to the skin. After an argument they decide to gamble for it. As the soldiers were wrestling and gambling over what was obviously a fine garment, was the woman who had made it standing there, thinking of the love that she had poured into it? The gospels do not attempt more than a spare description of the scene, but we can enter imaginatively into it. Those women loved this man as no man had ever been loved. One had borne him in her womb and suckled him at her breast. Of course, she had been warned that a sword would pierce her own heart, but there was no way of preparing for the sight of her own son being beaten through the streets of Jerusalem and then stripped naked on a cross. Apart from our Lady, two of the women were almost certainly particularly close to Jesus. The mother of 'the disciple whom Jesus loved', the one who had grasped most truly the real spirit and meaning of his work, must have felt a special bond to Jesus. Then there was Mary Magdalene whom he had healed, to whom he had given a purpose and a meaning, and whose devotion to him was total and extravagantly great. Mary Magdalene comes out of the gospel narrative shining. She it is, who is there at the garden tomb where they laid him and it is to her our Lord speaks on the first Easter Day. And John also was standing by, the only apostle whose courage equalled that of the women.

While this little scene is being acted out, our Lord looks down upon his mother and the little group at the foot of the cross. He is going into his last battle now; the time is approaching for his final struggle. So far his thoughts on the cross have only been for others, his enemies, his executioners: 'Father, forgive them'; for the penitent thief: 'Today you will be with me in paradise.' Before he entered into the deep inner struggle that awaited him (and we must remember that the struggle was not over for our Lord on the cross, it was really only reaching its climax), he performed one last act of human concern. He looks down and sees his blessed mother and the beloved disciple, and he delivers her into this man's keeping: 'Woman, behold your son; behold your mother.' And we read that he took her to his own home from that very hour. William Temple suggests that Jesus wanted John to take our Lady away that very moment, so she would be

50

spared the last awful struggle of his dying. We cannot be certain of this, but we know that John was there at the very end. Perhaps he took her to his home in Jerusalem and then hurried back to Calvary for the end.

It is strange that he handed his mother over in this way to John, because there was a group in the gospels called 'the brethren of our Lord'. Almost certainly they were not the brothers of Jesus. They were perhaps the sons of Joseph by a previous marriage. And the fact that Jesus delivered Mary into the care of John is strong evidence that Jesus was her only son. John was the son of our Lady's sister, Mary's closest blood relative. Our Lord, in his last act, gave his mother into his cousin's keeping. It was an act of filial piety; an act of concern, of love; the final putting of his own human affairs in order before his final journey.

One tradition tells us that our Lady stayed with John in Jerusalem and died aged 59. Another tradition tells us that he took her to Ephesus with him. There is absolute certainty that John lived until a great age in Ephesus where he either wrote or dictated his great gospel. Certainly, we know that our Lady was taken from that very hour into the keeping of the beloved apostle.

But the act was more than an act of simple provision for the welfare of his mother. In a deeper sense it was the creating of a new family; it was the beginning of the Church. Our Lady, in one sense, was the mother of the Church, which is itself a mother. Our Lord's last words to the world set up a new type of family, in which not blood, but charity would be the law that binds. So we must, when we meditate upon this third word of our Lord on the cross, think not only of his love for his mother, but also of the Church which is our mother. And since we are the Church, we are to be in some mysterious sense, mothers to others. We are to care in tenderness for those who are alongside us. The Church is to become a new kind of family, a new kind of fellowship. 'Behold your son; behold your mother.'

4

The Fourth Word

And when the sixth hour had come, there was darkness over the whole land until the ninth hour. And at the ninth hour Jesus cried with a loud voice, 'Elo-i, elo-i, lama sabach-thani?' which means, 'My God, my God, why hast thou forsaken me?' Mark 15:33–4

Now we come to the fourth and central word, recorded by Mark and Matthew, and I want to try to enter into its meaning by describing four events.

In Scotland the summer holidays have different names in different places. In Glasgow the holiday is called the 'Fair Fortnight'. In Edinburgh it is called the 'Trades Fortnight', because that is when all the trades stop and nothing happens for two weeks. I remember visiting a parishioner in Edinburgh who never forgot the Friday of a particular Trades Fortnight. That is when the holidays always started, and the works closed early. My parishioner was married, with two children under twelve years old, and they had been looking forward to going on holiday. She expected her husband home sometime in the middle of the afternoon on that Friday, but he never turned up; he did not come back. She waited for days. She could not go to his place of work, because it was closed for two weeks, but she did make inquiries, and she discovered that on the Friday when the works closed he had taken his vacation pay, every penny that was owed to him, and what was being saved for his retirement, and he had gone off to the south of England with another woman. He had not warned her. He had not informed anyone. She pieced the story together many months later after she had put a private detective on to it. She was torn in two by the information. She had no inkling that this was going to happen, that he could have carefully and coldly planned to walk out like this. There had been no forewarning, no preparation. She felt utterly forsaken.

The second story is about a friend of mine who worked in a mental hospital. There was a little girl there who did nothing but cry. She never spoke to anyone; she simply sat and cried. Finally, a brilliant and patient therapist discovered her story. She had lived alone with her mother, and one night, in the middle of the night, her mother gave birth to a baby, whom she promptly smothered. Then she wrapped the baby in an old blanket, and gave it to this child, who was then ten years old, and told her to take the baby to an abandoned building opposite and leave it there. The little girl obeyed, numb with horror. She was found hours later walking through the streets of the city with tears streaming down her face. The police found her, but she never spoke another word until the therapist managed to piece together the hideous reality that she had experienced. And what came out was the sense of forsakenness. This mother whom she had loved had gone into a place she did not understand. She had done hideous things and used her as an accomplice, so she felt forsaken by all she had ever loved.

I think also of a young married couple who were very much in love. He phoned up in the afternoon of their anniversary and said, 'I am taking you out to dinner tonight – get ready.' And then he never arrived home. Instead, a policeman arrived and said he had been killed on the way home in a hit-and-run accident. And she felt forsaken. She felt utterly crushed and numb.

Finally, let me give an experience of my own, less dramatic perhaps, but painful to me. When I had been a priest for five years, I realized that I no longer believed in God. I felt forsaken. Forsaken, even though I felt there was no God to forsake me, and for eighteen months I had to go through the motions of my faith, my priesthood, with no sense of the presence or reality of God.

These are patterns of forsakenness. To be forsaken is to be cut off from what gives your life meaning and beauty, what holds your life together, what makes you continue. And we come, in the fourth word, the most mysterious of the words, to an experience of forsakenness that nothing we have ever experienced can parallel, because it is on a unique level of dereliction. Nevertheless, some of the ways in which we have experienced the depths will give us a tiny clue, a tiny analogy, to the reality of what was going on up there on the cross at noon on that Friday. Our Lord defined himself by his closeness to God. He spoke of his *Father*. Often, he went apart and prayed to the Father, and always, he lived as in his sight. 'He who has seen me has seen the Father', 'I and the Father are one,' he said. There was a union between him and the Father which was total. They pulsed together. Our creed describes it as a total identity, 'being of one substance', and this communion with the Father, this being what the Father was (although in some sense he was emptied of it for our sake), had given him the courage to endure everything that the world threw at him. It had sustained him against every temptation to disobey his Father's will. Here he is now, forsaken by all in the world, even by his disciples. (Did he see Peter lurking out there in the crowd, Peter whom he loved, hanging back, shoulders and head down, unable to keep his eyes on Jesus?) Only a few women and his beloved John were there, but he could not reach them. He was only a few feet away, yet an infinity of distance separated him from them. And maybe by this time his mother had been taken away by John, as the great battle overwhelmed him. He was forsaken by all he had loved on earth, but sustained still by his Father. And, suddenly, the ground of his inner security disappears. God withdraws. The only thing that had kept Jesus together is taken away completely. He is forsaken. Suddenly, he feels absolutely bereft, even of God. The tense of the verb is very specific, it's an aorist, which is punctiliar in sense. It had happened in a moment. He was not describing a general condition, but a moment, like a stab or a thunderbolt. Nothing now sustains him. God goes forth from himself, un-Gods himself. We cannot enter into the heart of this word, this paradox, but maybe we can enter a few inches of the experience. God submitted himself to a forsakenness, a desertion of his own nature, for our sakes. This is the only time in the New Testament that Jesus calls God, 'God'. Not, this time, 'Abba', Daddy, Father, but *God*: 'My God, my God why hast thou forsaken me?'

How can we possibly enter this experience? Most of us experience forsakenness as something external to ourselves, however close the person who has forsaken us may have been. Is schizophrenia, perhaps, in some of its forms, an analogy? Something within your mind splits you apart. The experience of those who are going mad must approach this sense of absolute dereliction, a sense of being torn away from your own self. But we cannot

56

really enter into this experience by our minds alone. The poets help us best.

> O the mind, mind has mountains; cliffs of fall
> Frightful, sheer, no-man-fathomed. Hold them cheap
> May who ne'er hung there. Nor does long our small
> Durance deal with that steep or deep.
>
> (Gerard Manley Hopkins)

That was the experience of a man, but it may help us to approach the reality of that unique moment on the cross when God forsook his own Son. At any rate, here we are in the very heart of the Christian faith, and it is a mystery, dazzling in its blackness, though there are elements in it that we can, at least, apply our minds to.

Our Lord was identified totally with our experience. We know that one of the meanings of his life was a recapitulation of the whole human experience, of everything that had happened to humanity, only he went through it properly. Every level of abandonment he plumbed. He united himself to it all, to every desolate experience, every forsaken child. Certain strands of the New Testament say that at this moment he went into hell and harrowed it. Paul, in the Letter to the Ephesians, talks about the one who ascended also descending in love into the uttermost parts of the earth. These are phrases that come in flashes of vision, of insight and revelation. What they seem to mean is that our Lord went to the very bottom of the bottom of history, and became identified with it, uniting himself to it, and by so doing, somehow, redeemed it. By experiencing it, he transformed it, because in some sense the tragedy of human history is caused by our flight from responsibility. There is a sense in which we are ignorant; we do not know what we do. But there is another sense in which we have made our

57

own misery, and yet are impotent to help ourselves. Somehow we are brought to a judgement which we cannot bear, and he himself bears it in his own body on the tree. Now we know that it cannot overwhelm us for ever. That is why we meditate upon the cross, although, if we had seen it in its awful reality we would surely have shielded our eyes. This is the absolute centre, the total eclipse, the murder of God, which gave us life in a sense beyond defining. By the bearing of all sorrow, Christ saved the world. But no words can possibly explain the reality of that moment and its meaning. What we must do is to try to clutch the edges of this utter forsakenness. It will deepen our pity and compassion for others, but it will also afford us a moment of identity with the Son of God, who was forsaken by God in order to restore us to that place in God's heart, which we, in our ignorant wilfulness, had ourselves forsaken.

5

The Fifth Word

After this Jesus, knowing that all was now finished, said
(to fulfil the scripture), 'I thirst.' John 19:28

It is very near the end now. The period of absolute dereliction, which we thought about in the fourth word, that
central moment of the drama, cannot be measured in
time. Maybe he was in despair, in that forsaken place,
for two or three hours. We do know that he plumbed the
very depths of hell, the lowest parts of the earth. As Paul
says in Ephesians 4:9, 'In saying, "He ascended," what
does it mean but that he had also descended into the
lower parts of the earth?' And if we had been there, what
would we have seen? Nothing. There is a great silence
around the cross. Not a word is spoken after this word,
until the very end. But there was no lack of activity.
Indeed, it was at this time that the most intense activity
was taking place, because this was when Jesus was con-
fronting fully and finally the reality that tyrannized God's
creation, a confrontation that can only be put in the
language of struggle, of mystical conflict. This is what the
old hymn writers did: 'Sing, my tongue, the glorious
battle, sing the ending of the fray.' The old writers loved
that kind of warlike language. 'The royal banners forward
go, the Cross shines forth in mystic glow.' But it was a

strange battle. Doubtless his body was moving and twitching in the final agonies of death. One of the most hideous things about crucifixion was the constant battle for air. The poor victims had to push themselves up on their feet in order to get air into their lungs, and then they would slump down again in excruciating pain.

But the real battle, the glorious battle of which we sing, was fought in silence and blackness, in some deep place we can only visit in our minds. There was noise all around, but there was silence there. Then he emerges through it, and he gathers his strength for the final act of obedience, the final act of triumphant surrender. The last words on the cross are words of triumph, although they are poignant. As he comes out of this great, black pit, this forsaken place, this howling wilderness where he has been, he needs to refresh himself for his final act of strength. He is going now to drink the cup that at Gethsemane he prayed might pass from him. But he has fought the fight, he has kept the faith, he will now be faithful to the end.

There was a tradition, a merciful practice, that the victims of crucifixion were drugged. It was one of the social works, one of the acts of mercy of the wealthy ladies of Jerusalem. They would bring to the scene of crucifixion bowls of drugged wine in order to anaesthetize the poor victims who were dying hideous deaths. As we know, our Lord had refused the cup of drugged wine. He had refused it, presumably, because he wanted a clear head for battle, rather than to be in a stupor. But now that the battle is almost over, he wishes to be able to speak, and he cannot. His throat is parched. It must have been heartbreaking for those who loved him, seeing his mouth moving and his tongue dry and protruding, as they remembered how he had spoken; no man ever spoke the way this man spoke, we are told. Words that comforted, words that scorched, kind words, words of depth and beauty, no man spoke like this man. Now he can scarcely speak at all, yet he manages to croak, 'I thirst.' It was the only thing approaching a complaint that he said on the cross, and it was no complaint. He was about to take a practical step, because he wanted to prepare himself for his last words. How could he declare the glory that had been won if he could not speak? He wants to be able to speak, and the kindly soldiers (and one must remember this act, as well as their indifferent brutality) had with them a flask of cheap sour wine called by the gospel writers vinegar. It was the common soldiers' drink and they were probably drinking it as the afternoon wore on. One of them tips a little on to the end of a sponge (there was no way of holding a cup to the lips of a crucified man) and puts it on the end of a cane, a branch of hyssop. His mouth was probably within reach of an average man's arm, up there – his feet were only about eighteen inches above the ground. Jesus sucks a little of the sour wine.

But there is more to this act than the straightforward physical discomfort of thirst. Nothing in St John's gospel is simple. John always wants us to understand two or three things at the same time, and one of the things we must remember here, indeed ought to remember throughout our reading of the crucifixion narrative, is the prevailing background of the Old Testament. The central word of the cross is the first verse of Psalm 22: 'My God, my God, why hast thou forsaken me? Why art thou so far from helping me, from the words of my groaning?' To the first Christians that psalm irresistibly came to mind as they meditated on the Passion. They also heard Psalm 69: 'They gave me poison for food, and for my thirst they gave me vinegar to drink.' Our Lord himself was almost certainly meditating on the scriptures as he hung there. He knew them so well. He taught us how to use them, how to make them part of our very being, and this cry of his, 'I thirst', echoes much in the psalter.

As a hart longs for flowing streams,
  so longs my soul for thee, O God.
My soul thirsts for God,
  for the living God.
When shall I come and behold
  the face of God?
My tears have been my food
  day and night,
while men say to me continually,
  'Where is your God?' Psalm 42:1–4

And there was Psalm 63: 'O God, thou art my God, I seek thee, my soul thirsts for thee; my flesh faints for thee, as in a dry and weary land where no water is.' That is where our Lord had just been: in a dry and weary land where no water was, and he emerged from that dark wilderness with a thirst for God.

So, first of all, we must understand our Lord's real physical thirst and his need to slake his throat, so that he might proclaim the great words that were to end the drama of the cross. There is a deeper meaning to the verse, as well, because he emerged from the period of desolation with an enormous longing for God, a home-sickness for the Father, a heart-hunger. Have you never felt it? Have you never felt an enormous longing for God? You may not really ever have known him, you may doubt his very existence, yet your heart hungers. 'My soul thirsts for God, for the living God.' It comes to you sometimes in a dark church, in the quietness of dawn. It can come in the moorland. It can come when you see the first daffodils of spring. It can come in many ways: a sudden clutching of the heart, and a thirst for God. 'O God, thou art my God, I seek thee, my soul thirsts for thee, my flesh faints for thee.' After the great loss of God which he had experienced, our Lord experienced an overwhelming longing, the kind of longing that overwhelms us after a long separation from someone we love. 'I thirst for the living God.' Our Lord used this image of thirst many times, especially as recorded by John. He called himself a fountain of living waters. He said, 'Come to me, all who thirst. Out of me will flow streams of living water.' Jesus assuages our thirst for God, the dryness we wish to irrigate.

That is one of the meanings of this profound saying. But there is another kind of thirst. There is a thirst for the souls of men and women. There was an enormous tenderness in Jesus, though the proud and self-righteous never saw it. They only heard the words that cut like swords. But there were many others, such as the small and the despised, the children, who instinctively knew they could come to him; or the sinners who dared not lift up their eyes in the Temple, and who remained in the darkest parts of the church. 'Lord, be merciful to me, a sinner,' they humbly pleaded. The Roman soldiers, even, in their coarseness and rough honesty, our Lord always had a word for. All of these saw his grace, and felt his tenderness and strong love, and they were surprised at the effect he had on them, surprised by a sudden sense of longing for God. They would stop and catch themselves, and recognize that in this man's strong and grieving tenderness for them was something of the longing of God. What must it have been like to have looked into those strong, grieving eyes, and felt that love? No wonder that many of the poor sinners we read about in the New

Testament were smitten with great emotion and were given to bouts of tears, extravagant gestures of love, like the woman who anointed his feet and wiped them dry with the hair of her head. They were quite undone by the reality of the sense of the presense of God in Christ. They were smitten by the longing for them that poured out of him. He thirsted for them and they could sense it.

Literally, then, he thirsted. He wished to prepare himself for the final words. He also thirsted for God, figuratively. After the night, after the darkness, after the wilderness, he rediscovered a great longing, a great homesickness for the Father who had forsaken him. Finally, he thirsts for us, he longs for all of us to seek after him and find him, as we in our way thirst for him, and as we must thirst for the souls of other men and women, so that they too may know where to find the fountain of living waters.

6

The Sixth Word

When Jesus had received the vinegar, he said, 'It is finished'; and he bowed his head and gave up his spirit. John 19:30

I have a couple of portable typewriters which are a source of amusement to the parish secretaries. One is a tiny, thin little Olivetti, of which I am particularly fond, and about which they are particularly insulting. They call it an antique. They cannot understand why anyone would want to use an old non-electric typewriter. Yet I go on against their hard words and continue to use my tiny typewriter. The other one is an Adler which is a bit heavier and tougher, and much noisier. I keep that one in the basement of the rectory, and I keep the poor little Olivetti in my study at the church. But I did not always type my sermons. In the old days, before I learned to think on to a typewriter, I used to write them all out in longhand in big notebooks. I still have them all, great big notebooks full of handwritten sermons. Now, as I say, I no longer need to do that. But I like those volumes of old sermons. They are very disorganized, and they are not annotated. It is not possible to tell when a particular sermon was preached, unless you can discover some piece of internal evidence which allows you to date it. I like keeping these notebooks, and I shall always keep them. Although I am a great chucker-out of things, I will never chuck those out.

As well as having those volumes of my own sermons, I also have a complete set of another man's notebooks. My friend Isabella gave them to me. Unlike mine, these notebooks are well organized. One says on it: 'Aberdeen 1928: Epiphany; Lent; Easter; October; Angels; four sermons on "the World, the Flesh and the Devil".' In this book there are about forty sermons written out, and there is even a table of contents. I have a complete set of this priest's notebooks, and some of them are very dog-eared. I don't read them, however. I hold them on my lap, sort of flick through them and pick out the odd word here and there. They are a kind of sacrament to me. I get a strange sort of physical charge out of simply looking at them. Let me try to explain what I mean. I am not an old-sermon fetishist, nor do I nurse strange longings for old notebooks. I am fascinated, because these old sermons, sixty years old, and some even older than that, represent another priest's struggles with the reality of Christ. I find something moving and supportive and very wistful in these notebooks, as I think of that priest in his study in Aberdeen, all those years ago, wrestling with the same angels, meditating on the same Christ, conjuring the same history that I wrestle with, conjure up and meditate upon, in 1982. I get from these books a sense of the presence of Christ, the contemporary reality of Christ. He was real to this man as, in a strange way, he is real to me, as I wrestle with his elusive but overwhelming reality.

One man defined preaching as, 'a manifestation of the Incarnate Word, from the written word, by the spoken word'. The Incarnate Word, the Word of God, who became flesh two thousand years ago and walked the earth, was crucified under Pontius Pilate, and rose again from the dead, is made manifest today when the written words of the New Testament are made clear by the spoken words of the preacher. There is a chain of succession, an actualizing of the presence of Christ, which comes through this strange and mysterious activity of preaching. When it happens genuinely, Christ is made present: there is a revelation of the Incarnate Word. So preachers have to be solitary a lot of the time. You can meet the Incarnate Word best in solitude and Christ can then become manifest.

That is one reason why I look at this man's notebooks. I see him humbly, haltingly trying to put down on paper what can never really be put into words: the reality of the universal Christ, in Jerusalem two thousand years ago, in Aberdeen sixty years ago, and in Boston today. Preachers, for all their dumbness and confusion, nevertheless know that Christ is the real and living one. So our Good Friday meditations are not about a poignant defeat which we simply mourn over. They are really about a strange victory which released Christ for time and for eternity. On Good Friday we celebrate a great victory, for this man who was delivered into the hands of sinners who crucified him and put him to a terrible shame, was *by that very action* delivered unto glory.

We have to read these events on two levels. There is, first of all, the level of history, man's story, which is the bleak, terrible story of the mocking and doing to death of the poor man of Nazareth. The worst that we know in our human nature is paraded there. It is all that, and it remains that, and yet, at the same time, it is the work of God. There is an eternal chemistry, transmuting, transfiguring this transient horror into something that goes on for ever, and concerns us today. The defeat of Christ in time was also the triumph and glorification of God on a level that transcends and encompasses time. John uses two words almost interchangeably to describe this. He talks about the crucifixion and the glorification of Christ as one and the same thing. To the beholders, that death was the end, the ignominious defeat of a pretender. But to the eyes of faith it was the glorification of Christ, and this paradox, this two-dimensionality comes out perfectly in the sixth word, 'It is finished.' The word does not just mean, 'It's over, it's at an end.' It does mean that, of course, but John is always playing word games with us, because he wants us to ponder more deeply. His word *tetelestai* means it is *accomplished*, it is *fulfilled*, it is *achieved*. The word is often used by John:

> Jesus said to them, 'My food is to do the will of him who sent me, and to accomplish his work.' John 4:34
>
> But the testimony which I have is greater than that of John; for the works which the Father has granted me to accomplish, these very works which I am doing, bear me witness that the Father has sent me. John 5:36.

And in the great farewell discourse in the upper room we find it again: 'I glorified thee on earth, having accomplished the work which thou gavest me to do' (John 17:4). Almost for the last time, we find it before the fifth word in John 19:28, the same word, read throughout John's gospel: 'After this Jesus, knowing that all was now finished, said (to fulfil the scripture), "I thirst" ' (John 19:28).

The other evangelists say here that Jesus cried in a loud voice. This, according to John, is what he cried: 'It is *accomplished*. It is *finished*. The work I came to do is done.' God in Christ recapitulates man's history. The tragedy of man was his disobedience, his resistance to reality, his pettiness. The triumph of Christ is his obedience, his grasp of reality. In Christ our whole human experience was rerun, this time properly. By his obedience he justifies us. He reconstitutes our nature. The word the Fathers use to describe this is 'recapitulation'. Everything was done over again in him, the representative man.

So *tetelestai*, 'it is finished', is not a sad and wistful word. It is, rather, a shout of victory. In the words of the German theologian Krummacher: 'At these words you hear fetters burst, and prison walls falling down; barriers as high as heaven are overthrown, and gates which had been closed for thousands of years again move on their hinges.'

The fourth word was the moment of the assault of all that is *not* God against the will of God, and it was the moment when our Lord's most intense struggle began. But he overcame it. He burst through it by the power of his suffering and his obedient love, and he won the victory.

Paul uses a similar expression in 2 Timothy 4:6–8:

For I am already on the point of being sacrificed; the time of my departure has come. I have fought the good fight, I have finished the race, I have kept the faith. Henceforth there is laid up for me the crown of righteousness, which the Lord, the righteous judge, will award to me on that Day, and not only to me but also to all who have loved his appearing.

This is the end of the race for Christ. He bursts through the finishing tape. 'It is finished' is a word that should echo gloriously and never be muttered sorrowfully. Though it is a word, humanly speaking, of sadness and

69

parting, it is, in fact, the ultimate word of his triumph. 'It is accomplished.'

7

The Seventh Word

Then Jesus, crying with a loud voice, said, 'Father, into thy hands I commit my spirit!' And having said this he breathed his last. Luke 23:46

We should allow little lapse of time between the sixth and seventh words on the cross, between 'It is accomplished' and 'Into thy hands I commit my spirit'. After his triumphant claim, 'It is accomplished', Jesus bows his head, and hands over his spirit to God. The words again trap us. We normally think of this as a sort of final defeat, a last giving up and dying. We talk about struggling against death and finally giving in to it, but this is not at all the emphasis in our Lord's dying and in this account of it. The emphasis is all upon death as a *free act*. Jesus was not *killed*, he *died*. He gave up the spirit, he controlled the event. The words are important. John tells us Jesus *gave up* his spirit, he handed it over, or he dismissed it. There is no passivity in this dying. In this death the person who died was in control of the moment of death.

There is a major truth concealed in this apparently puzzling event. It is a truth which is controversial and can be expressed in different ways. According to certain thinkers, all human actions, including thought, are simply the result of a complex and predetermined mechanism.

The very thoughts that we think, the mind that moves, is simply the action of the brain – there is nothing beyond the physical mechanism. That is not the Christian view, of course, but it is not even a very sensible view. It certainly does not seem to be consistent with reality. Is it not odd to have brain waves that explain themselves to themselves? Who are they explaining to anyway? Behaviourism, physical determinism is pervasive in its influence, and it does affect how we understand ourselves.

It is not the most ancient or the most sensible tradition, and it is certainly not the scriptural tradition. According to the Christian tradition we are not simply bodies which manage to think and explain themselves. According to our tradition we are *incarnate spirits*. We are spirits expressing themselves in bodies. There is a reality which stands apart from the reality of the body, and should in fact direct and control the body. That is the theory. The fact is a little less straightforward. It is truer to say that we are spirits *learning* to control and guide the total reality of the person. Plato expressed it well in his parable of the charioteer, in which he said the horses were the appetites and the will was the charioteer. In an integrated, mature person the horses are driven in the direction of the charioteer's choosing. In a disordered and tumultuous nature, the horses plunge in different ways or they go only where they please. Plato taught from that parable that we must learn to integrate our personalities, so that our nature is moved at the behest of the governing principle of our personality which is *spirit*. In fact, we usually experience the opposite. We are usually driven by our passions and governed by our appetites. Rather than driving the chariot, we are usually driven by it.

Nevertheless, though we may be spirits who are only learning to be what we are supposed to be, this idea does correspond with our experience of the complexity of our personality. We are not simple, biological mechanisms. We are profounder and more complex than that. There is in us an experience of inwardness, an experience of transcendence of our own natures. The wrestling that we do with ourselves is witness to the fact. And we have seen something of it in others. We have seen in them the presence of a great strength and conviction which stands even against death itself, and the tyranny of the appetites and the passions. We see this picture of directed harmony and control at its ideal in Christ. Christ is the representative person. In Christ the physical and affective and mental natures were controlled by spirit, though not without struggle. We have hints in the New Testament of the great struggles of Christ as he sought to recapitulate, rerun properly for the first time, the history of our human nature.

As the sixth cry testifies, he accomplished what he was sent to do. He struggled, he wrestled, but ultimately his life went where he directed it. Compare that with what we know of ourselves: think of those gusts of temper which erupt in us from some boiler-house inside our unconscious; think of those rushes of sexual passion which overwhelm us; think of the ungovernable malice and bitterness of spirit, which often swell up within us. These are some of the forms which energy assumes in us, taking over and driving us far beyond our will.

So we develop a sort of 'victim' theory of our own nature, in which the pressure of the life spirit is felt to be vague, while the physical energies are powerful. And this is the way we think about our death. We assume that even at death we shall be a little piece of thistledown or flotsam. We shall be moved by events outside us. In fact, most people today die that way. They are not in control of their own dying. Death *happens* to them. It is not a thing they can do anything about.

That is not what we learn from Christ and those who have lived with something of his courage. For them life becomes something that they live, not something that simply happens to them. Death itself becomes a free, personal act. It is no longer an enemy which sneaks up on us. It is the final act of a person who controls his life. According to our Lord's example, death is something we can freely choose, indeed must choose, because it corresponds to the reality of personality as free spirit. Death has been defeated and robbed of its sting, and is something we can now make our own.

This is what he did. His last word was a giving back to God of that life which had come from God. 'Father, into thy hands I return my spirit.' This was the way of Christ, the free man, probably the only really free person, the only really complete person. So his death, as well as being a great and awful tragedy, is yet a triumph of the spirit, because it is controlled at every point, not by the human actors in the drama, by the executioners, by Pilate, by Herod, by Annas and Caiaphas; nor even by the very action of his own body with its cells and molecules, but by his own spirit. By freely choosing death and going through it obediently to the end, he reversed the tragedy of all dying. When Jesus had finished the work that the Father gave him to do, John tells us 'He bowed his head' as though to rest after labour. The word used can mean laying one's head gently on a pillow. There is a particularly poignant echo here, because our Lord had said of himself during the troubled years of his ministry, 'Foxes have holes, and birds of the air have nests; but the Son of man has no place to lay his head' (Matt 8:20). The word used here is the same word and he finally found where to lay his head – on the cross. He laid down his head and died. 'Father, into thy hands I commit my spirit.' This was the final free act of the only free man. By it we are set free to seek after that same freedom.

Bibliography

except where otherwise stated, place of publication is London

John Donne, Sermon 107, in *Sermons: Selected Passages*. (Oxford, Clarendon Press 1968), p. 107. Adapted by Eric Milner White, *My God My Glory*. (SPCK 1967), p. 27.

Gerald Manley Hopkins, 'No Worst, There is None', in *The Poems of Gerald Manley Hopkins*. (Oxford University Press 1967), p. 100.

G. A. Studdert Kennedy, 'Indifference' in *The Unutterable Beauty*. (Hodder & Stoughton 1947), p. 34.

Krummacher quoted by W. Graham Scroggie, *A Guide to the Gospels*. (Pickering & Inglis 1948), p. 588.

H. F. B. Mackay, *Assistants at the Passion*. (Milwaukee, Morehouse 1933), pp. 36, 37.

Edwin Muir 'The Killing', from *The Collected Poems of Edwin Muir 1921–1951*. (Faber 1952), p. 187.

Dorothy L. Sayers, *The Man Born to be King*. (Gollancz 1944), p. 310.

Helen Waddell, *Peter Abelard*. (Constable 1933), p. 290.